OPERAUP**CLOSE**

OperaUpClose present

PUCCINI'S
LA FANCIULLA
DEL WEST
WEST END GIRL

A new version by Robert Chevara & Kfir Yefet

First performed at the King's Head Theatre on 31 January 2012

PUCCINI'S
LA FANCIULLA DEL WEST
WEST END GIRL

CAST

MINNIE
LAURA PARFITT, DEMELZA STAFFORD

'VIK' JOHNSON
BEN THAPA, ADAM CROCKATT

JACK ROCK
TOM STODDART, TOM BULLARD

NIK
EDMUND HASTINGS

SONORA
SIMON MEADOWS

YURI
MATTHEW STIFF

PRODUCTION AND CREATIVE TEAM

Director & Librettist	Robert Chevara
Librettist	Kfir Yefet
Musical Director	John Gibbons
Set Designer	Nicolai Hart Hansen
Costume Designer	Jonathan Lipman
Lighting Designer	Andrew May
Scenic Artist	Gregor Donnelly
Assistant Director	Holly Aston
Assistant Musical Director	Christopher Stark
Costume Assistant	Amy Gibson
Video Design	Richard Jephcote
Producers	Dominic Haddock Rachel Lerman
Stage Manager	Lee Davies
Assistant Stage Manager	Greg Eldridge
Artistic Directors **OperaUpClose**	Adam Spreadbury-Maher Robin Norton-Hale

ROBERT CHEVARA
(DIRECTOR/LIBRETTIST)

Robert was born in London and has written and directed plays, opera, television and film. In 2009 he directed *La Voix Humaine* to great acclaim in Stockholm. Robert directed *Top Girls* by Caryl Churchill for the English Theatre, Berlin, and worked with the company again on a stage reading of *Cheech* or *The Chrysler Guys Are In Town* by Francois Letourneau. He was invited to New Zealand Opera to direct *Madama Butterfly* and to Banff, Canada to direct the world premiere of Pascal Dusapin's *To Be Sung*. Robert directed *The Rake's Progress*, *Carmen*, *Fidelio* and *Macbeth* for English Touring Opera, for whom Robert was Director of Productions from 1997-2001. He directed an award-winning *Powder Her Face* for Ystad Opera Festival in Sweden, Handel's *Radamisto* and *Lothario* for the Royal College of Music, *The Tales of Hoffman*, *Les Dialogues Des Carmelites* and Dvorak's *The Cunning Peasant* for Guildhall School of Music & Drama and the 1999 National Opera Studio's London Showcase. He was co-director on the BBC2 television series of Marscher's *The Vampire* which won the Prix Italia. He also directed *Hamlet* and *Mary Rose* by J.M. Barrie at Theatre Space, Covent Garden and choreographed *Les Noces* at the Banff Centre for the Arts.

Recent projects include a film/performance/installation collaboration with the artist Victor Burgin for the London Symphony Orchestra's Centre at St Luke's, Old Street and the hugely successful devised play with music, *Fair!* In Rayleigh High Security Women's Prison for the National Youth Theatre. In 2010 Robert directed *Purity and Desire* and a new play *The Bench* by punk legend Bertie Marshall at The Drill Hall, London.

Robert was awarded a Churchill Fellowship in 1995 and the Japanese Government's cultural study award in 1997. Mid-Wales Opera won the Prudential Award for his production of *Carmen*. www.robertchevara.com.

KFIR YEFET
(LIBRETTIST)

Kfir is a writer/director whose first professional short film, *It's Not Unusual*, starring Meera Syal, met with great international acclaim and won a BAFTA for Best Short Film.

His extensive work as a theatre director includes a collaboration with the choreographer Amir Hosseinpour at the Almeida Theatre - *Is That All There Is?* - featuring Liliane Montevecchi, which later transferred to New York's La Mama Theatre and won a New York Critics Award. Other theatre work includes Stravinsky's *The Soldier's Tale* with Frances de la Tour and Jonathan Lunn, *Fantaisie Nocturne* (Angharad Rees, Turtle Key), *The Snow Queen* (QEH), Berio's *Recital 1* featuring Teresa Cahill, and the European premiere of *Shimmer* by John O'Keefe at the Mermaid Theatre.

Kfir also directed Ibsen's *A Doll's House* in a new version by Zinnie Harris at the Donmar Warehouse (2010 Olivier Awards Best Actress nomination - Gillian Anderson).

Other work includes a screenplay of *The Houdini Girl*, based on the novel by Martyn Bedford, and an adaptation of Mark Behr's novel *The Smell of Apples*.

JOHN GIBBONS
(MUSICAL DIRECTOR)

John studied at Queens' College, Cambridge, the RAM and the RCM, winning awards as conductor, pianist and accompanist. He has conducted at South Africa's Spier Festival, the Crested Butte Festival, Colorado, Walton's First Symphony in Romania and Malcolm Arnold's Fourth Symphony at the 2011 Cesis Festival, Latvia. John has conducted numerous acclaimed shows for Opera Holland Park and most of the major British orchestras including the RPO, CBSO, LPO, BBCSO and Philharmonia. John is Principal Conductor of Worthing Symphony Orchestra, the professional orchestra of West Sussex, presenting concerts in the acoustically acclaimed Assembly Hall. John devised and ran two national Karl Jenkins tours and made the authorised small-scale version of Karl's *Stabat Mater*. His 2006 reduction of Walton's *Troilus & Cressida* for Opera St Louis, drew much critical praise in the USA.

John is passionate about British music and his recording of Arthur Benjamin's string concertos on Dutton has been enthusiastically received. He is chairman of the British Music Society and a William Alwyn Foundation Trustee. His renowned communication with audiences was recognized in a Fellowship from the Royal Society of Arts. His own compositions include a BFI film score, *Fixer's Galop* for WSO as well as choral works for Clifton Cathedral, where he is Choral Director. www.johnsgibbons.com

NICOLAI HART HANSEN (SET DESIGN)

Work includes: *Desert Boy*, *An African Cargo* (Nitro Theatre), *The Lily of The Valley* (ROH2), *Hetty Feinstein's Wedding Anniversary* (New End), *Idomeneo*, *Eugene Onegin* (Hampstead Garden Opera), *Orpheo* (Scarlett Opera), *Playing the Victim* (Royal Court Theatre), *Watership Down* (design associate to Melly Still) *Some Girls are Bigger than Others* (Lyric Hammersmith), *Private Fears in Public Places* (Royal Theatre Northampton), *An Explosion* (BAC), *Medea in Jerusalem* (Rattlestick, New York) *Here be Monsters* (Rejects Revenge), *Behind the Iron Mask* (Duchess Theatre), *Three Days of Rain*, *Winter Under the Table*, *The Mapmakers Sorrow* (Copenhagen), *Company*, *The Kitchen*, *Dancing at Lughnasa* (Embassy Theatre), *Mine* (Kaos Theatre), *Natural Inclinations* (Finborough), *War and Love Season*, *More Lies about Jerzy*, *Alice Virginia*, *The Crystal Den*, *The Last Obit* (New End), *Dolores* (Arcola Theatre), *Japes* (Not the National Theatre), *Shopping and Fucking*, *Demons* (Linbury Studio) *La Bohème* (European Chamber Opera), *Woyzeck* (design assistant to Robert Wilson) *2012: Reunion* (Jermyn Street Theatre) *Tremor in the Bones* (Rambert Dance Company) *Habe Kein Angst* (Copenhagen). Nicolai trained at Central School of Speech and Drama and The Slade School of Fine Art, and teaches and lectures in theatre design and scenography. http://www.nicolaiharthansen.blogspot.com

JONATHAN LIPMAN
(COSTUME DESIGN)

Theatre includes *Purity and Desire* (Drill Hall London); *The Country Girl* (West End, national tour); *Larkrise to Candleford, The Haunting, Jekyll and Hyde: The Musical;* and *Keeler* (national tours). Theatre as Associate Costume Designer includes *Richard III* (Old Vic, BAM, world tour); *Dr Dee* (Manchester International Festival, ENO London. Jonathan is a director of Angels Costume, London and has supplied costumes to theatre, opera, television and film productions, collaborating with the industry's leading costume designers, producers, directors and actors.

ANDREW MAY
(LIGHTING DESIGN)

Andrew May studied and trained in lighting design from a very early age. As well as previously working for a number of theatre companies, large and small he has spent the last six years working with Glyndebourne Opera as an assistant lighting designer. His Lighting Design credits include *Così fan tutte* - LA Opera (Los Angeles), *Of Water and Tears, Night Pieces, Yellow Sofa, Renard & Mavra* and *La Descente d'Orphée aux Enfers* – Jerwood Chorus Development Programme (Glyndebourne/LPO), *Who am I* – Glyndebourne Youth Opera (Tête à Tête Festival), Ceremony of Carols – Glyndebourne Youth Opera (Glyndebourne) and twelve annual productions for the Winchester School of Performing Arts. Throughout his career he has worked alongside some of the world's leading lighting designers in opera, including Paule Constable, Mark Henderson, Robin Carter, Robert Bryan

and Peter van Praet, whilst assisting on productions of *Albert Herring, Tristan und Isolde, Così fan tutte, Don Giovanni* and *The Rake's Progress* for Glyndebourne Festival Opera. He also relit Peter Van Praet's production of *L'Incoronazione di Poppea* and Bernd Purkrabek's *Don Pasquale* for touring with Glyndebourne On Tour. His forthcoming productions include *Le nozze di Figaro* and *Yellow Sofa* – Glyndebourne.

HOLLY ASTON
(ASSISTANT DIRECTOR)

Holly graduated from Lancaster University with a First Class BA (Hons) degree in Theatre Studies and has also trained at École Internationale de Théâtre Jacques Lecoq in Paris. She has written and directed plays and worked as an actress and theatre education practitioner.

Directing credits include: *Oedipe* for a site-specific performance in Paris, Co-director for *Twelfth Night* at the Kwai Tsing Theatre in Hong Kong, Assistant Director for *Rosencrantz and Guildenstern Are Dead* at the Sai Wan Ho Theatre in Hong Kong, Movement Director for *Julius Caesar* at the Kwai Tsing Theatre, Assistant Director for *Arcadia* at Hong Kong Arts Centre and Assistant Director for *The Madness of King George III* at the Edinburgh Fringe Festival.

In 2010 she wrote the script adaptations for Bram Stoker's *Dracula* and Charles Dickens' *Great Expectations* for the Page to Stage Season at the Sai Wan Ho Theatre.

Acting credits include: Nerissa in *The Merchant Of Venice* at the Hong Kong Arts Centre, The Reporter in *Yellow Face*, directed by David Henry

Hwang at Hong Kong University, Rita in *Educating Rita* at the Hong Kong Arts Centre, Constanze in *Amadeus* at the Edinburgh Fringe Festival, Deviser and performer in *Your Guide To Death (is beautiful)* for Drunken Chorus Productions' UK tour, Lady Macbeth in *Macbeth* at the Edinburgh Fringe Festival and Deviser and Performer (whilst in training) in *Scene by Scene*, directed by Tim Etchells at The Nuffield Theatre in Lancaster.

Holly is currently Resident Trainee Director with OperaUpClose at the King's Head Theatre and is thrilled to be joining the company as full-time General Manager from February 2012.

CHRISTOPHER STARK
(ASSISTANT MUSICAL DIRECTOR)

Christopher spent four years at Trinity College, Cambridge, completing a BA and a MusB focusing on the music of James MacMillan whilst a choral scholar. After various operatic roles in Europe and Japan as a treble, he played the cello in the National Youth Orchestra. Conducted opera productions include, with the Cambridge University Opera Society, Britten's *The Turn of the Screw*, Debussy's *Pelléas et Mélisande*, Stravinsky's *The Rake's Progress*, Walton's *The Bear*, along with Mozart's *Der Schauspieldirektor* and Joel Rust's *Nauset*. Last summer he conducted performed Britten's *Albert Herring* on a tour with Shadwell Opera ending at Opera Holland Park, along with Stravinsky's *The Rite of Spring* on top of a Peckham car park. With the Cambridge University Music Society and Symphony Orchestra he has conducted Mahler's Fourth, Brahms's First and Sibelius's Fifth and Seventh Symphonies. He will be conducting

Kate Whitley's opera *Unknown Position* at the King's Head as part of OperaUpClose after performances at the Edinburgh Fringe Festival and at the Cockpit Theatre, Marylebone. In 2008 he formed The Kallion Ensemble, an orchestra with a focus on smaller scale twentieth-century repertoire.

DOMINIC HADDOCK (PRODUCER)

Dominic graduated in Theatre & Performance Studies from the University of Warwick. He pursued a career in the city, co-founding a successful business development agency, before returning to the theatre. He has worked in various capacities for Headlong Theatre; Really Useful Theatre; Out of the Blue Productions; The Onassis Programme; Iris Theatre; and The Associated Studios. Production credits include *Romeo & Juliet* (Iris Theatre); *The Wind in the Willows* (Iris Theatre); *The Barber of Seville* (OperaUpClose); *Madam Butterfly* (OperaUpClose); *Pagliacci* (OperaUpClose); *I Never Get Dressed Till After Dark On Sundays* (The Cock Tavern Theatre); *A Cavalier For Milady* (The Cock Tavern Theatre & The Jermyn Street Theatre); *The Turn of the Screw* (OperaUpClose); *Manifest Destiny* (OperaUpClose); *Constance* (King's Head Theatre); *La Bohème* (OperaUpClose) and now *La Fanciulla del West* (OperaUpClose). Dominic is the Executive Producer of OperaUpClose & the King's Head Theatre.

RACHEL LERMAN
(PRODUCER)

Rachel has been with OperaUpClose since January 2011. Before producing *La Fanciulla del* West, she was Assistant Producer on *Madam Butterfly, The Barber of Seville* and *Pagliacci* at the King's Head Theatre, and Associate Producer on *Don Giovanni* at Soho Theatre. She has previously worked with Belt Up Theatre as a Stage Manager on their productions of *Metamorphosis* at the National Student Drama Festival and *A Clockwork Orange* at the York Theatre Royal. She also writes, performs and produces for comedy group Four Sad Faces, with whom she has worked on two BBC radio programmes and three Edinburgh Fringe Festival shows. She graduated from the University of York in 2009 with a First Class BA (Hons) in History.

ADAM SPREADBURY-MAHER
(ARTISTIC DIRECTOR, OPERAUPCLOSE)

Adam is an award-winning director and producer, originally trained as a tenor in Australia. Adam founded the Cock Tavern Theatre in 2009 and won The Peter Brook Dan Crawford award. He founded OperaUpClose with Ben Cooper and Robin Norton-Hale, producing *La Bohème* at the Cock Tavern and Soho Theatres, winner of the Olivier Award for Best Opera.

Directing highlights: Louis Nowra's *Cosi* and Daniel Reitz's *Studies For A Portrait* (White Bear), Peter Gill's *The York Realist* and *The Sleepers Den* (Riverside Studios), Hannie Rayson's *Hotel Sorrento* and a new play by Edward Bond, *There Will Be More* (Cock Tavern Theatre), and in Australia Jonathan Harvey's *Beautiful Thing* and Joe Orton's *Loot*. For

OperaUpClose he directed *Madam Butterfly* (King's Head).

Producing highlights: Jack Hibberd's *A Stretch of the imagination*, the hit musical *Pins and Needles*, the world premiere of Tennessee Williams' *I Never Get Dressed Till After Dark On Sundays*, and the landmark six-play edward Bond retrospective (Cock Tavern Theatre), *The Coronation of Poppea* and *Don Giovanni* (Soho Theatre). In 2010 Adam became Artistic Director of the King's Head and won Best Artistic Director in the Fringe Report Awards. In 2012 he has been nominated for Best Director in the Off-West End Awards and will direct the London premiere of Arnold Wesker's *Denial* to celebrate the playwright's 80th birthday, and his new 4-singer version of *Tosca* for Malmö Opera before an autumn production at the King's Head. Follow him on twitter @ Spreadbury

ROBIN NORTON-HALE
(ARTISTIC DIRECTOR, OPERAUPCLOSE)

Robin founded OperaUpClose alongside Adam Spreadbury-Maher and Ben Cooper in October 2009. Her directing credits for OperaUpClose, all in her own new English translations, are *La Bohème* (Soho, Cock Tavern & King's Head Theatres, winner of the 2011 Olivier Award for Best Opera and the Whatsonstage.com Award for Best Off-West End Production), *Don Giovanni* (Soho Theatre) and *The Barber of Seville (or Salisbury)* (King's Head). Other directing credits include *The Taming of the Shrew* (Southwark Playhouse), *Visions of Kerouac* (Half Moon Theatre), *Best Man Speech* (UK tour), *Pick 'n' Myths* (Lyric Theatre Hammersmith and UK tour), *Spirit* of Vienna (English Touring Opera), *Live Canon* (Northcott and Greenwich Theatres), *Happy Campers* (site specific performances at Montagu Close), *Pimpinone* (Colourhouse Theatre), and a revival of James Conway's production of *Ariodante* for ETO. She was Associate Director on *Cloudcuckooland*, a new musical by Stephen Sharkey and Alex Silverman (UK and international tour); Assistant Director credits include *Sweet Charity* (Theatre Royal, Drury Lane), *Katya Kabanova* and *The Seraglio* (both ETO). In autumn 2012 she will direct her own new version of *Let's Make an Opera* and Britten's *The Little Sweep* for Malmö Opera House, Sweden. Follow Robin on twitter @robinnortonhale.

LAURA PARFITT (MINNIE)

Born in Risca, South Wales Laura Parfitt began her studies at the Welsh College of Music and Drama and then at the Royal Academy of Music, completing her studies at Dennis O'Neill's Cardiff International Academy of Voice. She has won numerous prizes including an award from the BBC, the Dame Eva Turner Prize for dramatic soprano, the Harriet Cohen Major Prize and the Sir Geraint Evans Scholarship. Since graduating, Laura's engagements have included the title role in *Anna Bolena* and Donna Elvira *Don Giovanni* (English Touring Opera), Adina *L'Elisir d'amore* and Rose Maybud *Ruddigore* for (Opera Della Luna and Ilford Festival Opera), Gretchen *The Poacher* (Buxton Festival), Rosina *Il barbiere di Siviglia* (Welsh National Opera) and Berta (Scottish Opera). She sings regularly as a concert soloist and has performed at prestigious venues including the Royal Albert Hall, the Royal Festival Hall and Cadogan Hall. She has shared the concert platform and opera stage with many acclaimed singers including Rebecca Evans, Susan Bullock and Colin Lee. She has appeared on BBC Radio 3's *In Tune*, and has made several television appearances including a gala concert with Dame Kiri Te Kawana and Dennis O'Neill. Laura's future engagements include her first *Tosca* in summer 2012.

DEMELZA STAFFORD (MINNIE)

Demelza studied at The Guildhall School of Music and Drama and The Royal College of Music before continuing her studies privately under the tuition of her teachers and coaches including Nelly Miricioiu, Ameral Gunson and Mark Packwood. She made her debut in 2009 as Violetta Valery, *La Traviata* (New Cornwall Opera) at The Minack theatre and has since performed the role for Candlelight and Chelmsford Opera as well as covering it for New Devon Opera. In the summer of 2011 Demelza returned to the stunning Minack Theatre to make her first appearances as Cio Cio San in *Madame Butterfly* (New Cornwall Opera). Recent roles also include Dido *Dido and Aeneas* (Park Opera), Elisabetta *Maria Stuarda* (Operatique) and Mother *Hansel and Gretel* (GSMD). Among other recital and concert appearances in England and Germany, Demelza gave the UK premier of Jake Heggie's song cycle, *Natural Selection* and is due to premier his one act opera, *At The Statue of Venus* in the near future.

BEN THAPA
('VIK' JOHNSON)

Ben Thapa studied at the Guildhall School of Music and Drama and the Royal College of Music, London. In addition to his most recent sponsorship from the Wagner Society, Ben has been supported by a number of major bursars, including the Musicians Benevolent Fund and the Levenshulme Trust.

Recent performances include Vanya Kudrjash in Scottish Opera's touring production of *Kátya Kabanová, Mat of the Mint* The Beggar's Opera for the Royal Opera at the Linbury Theatre, First Prisoner & Florestan (cover) *Fidelio* and Armed Man & Tamino (cover) for Garsington Opera, Siegmund (cover) *Die Walküre* for the Wagner Society with David Syrus and Max (cover) *Der Freischütz* for the Opéra Comique, Paris. Michael *Manga Sister*, a new opera by Harry Blake, directed by Martin Constantine for LIVEARTSHOW and Corebo *Didone* at the GSMD.

Ben is also in demand on the concert platform across an unusually wide range of repertoire for a young singer. He has performed at venues including the Royal Albert Hall, Cadogan Hall and King's College, Cambridge with conductors including Sir John Eliot Gardiner, Brian Kay.

Next year Ben will study with Dennis O'Neill at the Wales International Academy of Voice in Cardiff.

ADAM CROCKATT ('VIK' JOHNSON)

Adam Crockatt hails from London, England, and studied at The Guildhall School of Music and Drama, under the tutelage of Adrian Thompson.

Recent work includes singing 4ème Jeune Homme in Wexford Opera's production of *La Coeur De Célimène* (Thomas), as well as chorus for their production of *Maria* (Statkowski). He also recently performed as Don Ottavio in OperaUpClose's production of *Don Giovanni*.

Previous work includes singing Laurie in Mark Adamo's new opera *Little Women* (Banff Opera), chorus for Grange Park Opera's productions of *Rigoletto* and *Tristan Und Isolde*, Head Oompa Loompa in the European Premiere of *The Golden Ticket* (Wexford Festival Opera), where he also performed in the chorus for Mercadante's *Virginia*.

In his spare time he writes pop music, singing and playing guitar in his band, Everybody Be Cool.

TOM STODDART (JACK ROCK)

A graduate of Trinity college of music, Tom is fast establishing himself as an opera and concert soloist. He has recently performed the role of Leporello *Don Giovanni* for OperaUpClose at the Soho Theatre and Paul in *Les Enfants Terribles* (Phillip Glass) as part of the Grimeborn festival, for which he received favourable reviews in all the major national newspapers. His recent solo concert work includes; Mozart *Requiem*, Haydn *Nelson Mass*, Rossini's *Petit Messe Solennelle*), Duruflè *Requiem*, *Carmina Burana* and *St John Passion*. Tom is currently creating the role of Chandler in comedy central's *Friends-The Opera*. Tom currently studies with Robert Dean.

TOM BULLARD
(JACK ROCK)

Tom Bullard trained at King's College, Cambridge. For OperaUpClose, he has sung Figaro in *The Barber of Seville* and Dandini in *La Cenerentola*. For Opera South, he has sung Peter Ivanov in *Peter the Great*, and covered Piquillo in *La Périchole*, as well as gala performances for New Year 2011, and the 2011 Summer Gala with Ann Murray. Other roles include Max in a new opera,

Demon Lover, for Grimeborn Opera, the Soldier in *Alban* for Alban Opera, Smirnov in *The Bear* for Minotaur Music Theatre, Piquillo (cover) in *La Périchole* for Opera South, Macheath in *The Beggar's Opera*, and Adonis in *Venus and Adonis*. Tom made his debut with the London Symphony Orchestra in Steve Reich's *The Desert Music* and Richard Einhorn's *Voices of Light*, and was the baritone soloist in Steve Reich's *The Cave*, with Ensemble Modern, all in October 2011. He has performed for private functions at Dartmouth House and The Ritz.

Tom was a member of the Swingle Singers from 2001 to 2008, and was the Musical Director from 2004. Under his direction the group toured through Europe, the USA, Asia, South America and New Zealand, performing with the world's finest orchestras and conductors, including with Maggio Musicale, Florence, and the Vienna Philharmonic, both conducted by Zubin Mehta, the Accademia di Santa Cecilia under Antonio Pappano, the Orquesta Nacional de España under Josep Pons, and the Royal Liverpool Philharmonic Orchestra under Carl Davis.

Tom currently teaches Singing at Westminster Under School and St Paul's School, and is also Musical Director of The Allegri Singers.

EDMUND HASTINGS (NICK)

Having sung at King's College, Cambridge and New College, Oxford, Edmund currently studies at the Royal Academy of Music with Ryland Davies and Dominic Wheeler, where he is the holder of the Nan Copeland Award and the Norman McCann Scholarship, and is generously supported by the Michael James Music Trust, the Sir Richard Stapley Educational Trust and the Musician's Benevolent Fund.

Recent opera roles include Arioch Belshazzar (Theatre du Capitole, Toulouse, René Jacobs), Jupiter *Semele* (Hampstead Garden Opera), Lysander *Midsummer Night's Dream* (Rosslyn Chapel), Tenor 1 in Frank Martin's *Le Vin Herbé* and Male Chorus *The Rape of Lucretia* and Don Basilio *Le Nozze di Figaro*, both for RAM opera scenes. Future plans include Cinea *Cajo Fabricio* (cover) for the London Handel Festival, and chorus for Garsington Opera this summer (*Don Giovanni* and *La Périchole*).

Edmund made his concert debut in the Barbican in 2008, under Laurence Cummings. His concert appearances in 2011 included Mendelssohn *Paulus* (St Martin's, Dorking), Haydn *Seasons* (Swindon Choral Society), Bach *St John Passion* (Fiori Musicali), Monteverdi *Vespers* (also Fiori), Mozart *Requiem* (St Martin in the Fields) and Handel *Jephtha* (Felsted Choral Society). Future concert plans include *St Matthew Passion* (arias) in Israel and Ireland, and the *St John Passion* (evangelist) in Norfolk and London.

SIMON MEADOWS (SONORA)

Australian born Baritone Simon Meadows studied at The Victorian College of the Arts, Melbourne graduating with a BA(Music) and then going on to do a Grad Dip(Opera). He performed in recitals and sang roles in Opera Studio productions. The Speaker and 2nd Armed Man *The Magic Flute*, Count Almaviva *The Marriage of Figaro* Guglielmo *Così fan tutte*, Marco Gianni *Schicchi* Junius *The Rape of Lucretia* and Tchelio in *The Love of Three Oranges* (VCA Opera Studio)

The Gaoler in *Tosca*, Messenger *La Traviata*, Claudio *Beatrice and Benedict*, Ko Ko *The Mikado*, Don Alhambra *The Gondoliers* (Opera Australia). David in Samuel Barber's *A Hand of Bridge*, Dancairo and Morales Bizet's *Carmen*, Silvio *I Pagliacci*, Tarquinius *The Rape of Lucretia* (Lyric Opera Melbourne). Marcello *La Boheme* and Demetrius *A Midsummer Night's Dream* (Co Opera South Australia). Simon portrayed the World War One British Poet Rupert Brooke in Nicholas Vines' Green Room Award winning world premier Opera *The Hive* (Chambermade Opera). Musiklehrer *Ariadne auf Naxos*, Jimmy in Stuart Greenbaum's *The Parrot Factory* and worked on a collaboration with the Australian Ballet singing the Baritone solo in Faure's *Requiem* (Victorian Opera). Concert engagements have included Dvorak's *Te Deum* (Stonnington Symphony)and dramatic Cantata *The Spectre's Bride*(Willoughby Symphony), Schubert's *Mass in G*, Bach's *Wachet Auf cantata*(Victoria Chorale), Mozart's *Requiem* (Sydney Philharmonia) Orff's *Carmina Burana* (Melbourne Philharmonia) Handel's *Messiah*(Victoria Chorale), Haydn's *Nelson Mass* (National Boys Choir), Vaughan Williams *Five Mystical Songs* (Melbourne Uni Chorale), *A Sea Symphony* (Willoughby Symphony) *Serenade to Music* (Victoria Chorale), Mahler's *Kindertotenlieder* and Beethoven's *Choral Fantasia* (Monash Symphony).

MATTHEW STIFF (YURI)

Matthew Stiff (Bass/Baritone) was born in Grimsby and studied at the University of Huddersfield for both his BMus (Hons) and MA (Perf). He went on to study atthe Guildhall School of Music and Drama with support from the Wingate Foundation, the Worshipful Company of Goldsmiths and a Maidment Scholarship administered by the Musicians Benevolent Fund. He graduated with distinction from the Guildhall opera course in 2011. His operatic roles include Pietro d'Visantis *L'assedio di Calais,* Superintendent Budd *Albert Herring*, Tongo *La Spinalba*, Le Geôlier/Monsieur Javelinot *Dialogues des Carmélites* and King René*Iolanta* (Guildhall School of Music and Drama), Antonio *Le nozze di Figaro* (Vignette Productions), Sergeant of Police *The Pirates of Penzance* (Grimsby Operatic Society), Marchese d'Obigny *La Traviata* (Chelsea Opera Group), Don Magnifico *La Cenerentola* (Clonter Opera), Charon *Eurdice* and Figaro *Le nozze di Figaro* (British Youth Opera) and King Balthazar*Ahmal and the Night Visitors* (Iford Arts). Future engagements include Prince Gremin *Eugine Onegin*, Surin (cover) *Queen of Spades* (Nevill Holt/Grange Park Opera) and Pistola *Falstaff* (Chateau Berbiguieres). He continues to study with John Evans.

PATRONS AND SPONSORS

We are only able to carry on producing work of the quality we strive for through fundraising activities, our patrons and sponsors and by selling tickets through our box office.
Our Patrons and Sponsors support us with a range of valuable contributions which allow us to continue our work, acquire particular assets we need and to fund productions.

FOUNDER PATRON

In November 2010 we were pleased to announce that Tower Leasing Ltd became our Founder Patron providing much needed financial support on an annual basis on top of providing us with a much needed baby grand piano. Arranging finance for a variety of organisations to allow them to acquire much needed capital equipment to help their businesses grow, Tower understand the importance of having the right assets in place at the right time and are now using their expertise through a variety of methods to help OperaUpClose do the same.

FOUNDER SPONSOR

Buff Snacks, which supplies delicious snacks at theatres throughout the UK, have supported us a great deal at the King's Head Theatre.
Buff Snacks are the sponsors of our opera programme at the King's Head Theatre. Buff Snacks have also donated us a yearly subscription for our accounting software.

Sponsors

The Lord Wolseley Pub generously supports us with rehearsal space

St Augustine Church generously supports us with rehearsal space

Islington Pianos generously supports us with technical advice and support

Become a friend of **Opera**Up**Close**. . .

Become a Friend   £25 per year
Receive our weekly *What's On* newsletter
Acknowledgment on our website

Key to the Stage Door   £150 per year
Receive our monthly friends & patrons' newsletter
Acknowledgment on our website & in programmes
Invitations to patrons' events

Key to the Dressing Room   £500 per year
Receive our monthly friends & patrons' newsletter
Acknowledgment on our website & in programmes
Invitations to patrons' events
Priority ticket booking

Key to the Opera House   £1,000 per year
Receive our monthly friends & patrons' newsletter
Acknowledgment on our website & in programmes
Priority ticket booking
Invitations to patrons' events
Free programmes for OperaUpClose productions
Reserved seats at any performance

There are other ways in which you can support OperaUpClose:

Sponsor the Costumes for our production of *Carmen*   £2,000
You can sponsor all the costumes for our production of *Carmen*, opening in April 2012. Come along and see our singers in the boots that you bought.

Tune the Piano for a year   £3,000
Our musical directors give our beautiful baby grand piano a good old bash every night. Looking after it and making sure it sounds good for every performance is an expensive job. Would you like to sponsor the cost of a year's worth of piano tuning?

Stage Facelift   £5,000
We love our theatre, but 40 years of performances have taken their toll and the poor thing needs a bit of work. We have plans to deck out the auditorium, fix the roof, stop the stage sinking, plaster the walls etc and we'd love your help.

Singers' Fees for a Production   £10,000
How would you like to invest in the future of a small group of young singers? Sponsor the performance fees for the cast of our production of *Carmen* in April.

OPERAUP**CLOSE**

OperaUpClose is dedicated to presenting new, difficult and classic operas in intimate spaces with world-class trained singers and directors, bringing opera to life for diverse audiences and offering the extraordinary opportunity to experience the dramatic and musical event of opera up close.

We are completely unfunded, and rely on our friends to support us and allow us to continue our work. *La Bohème* was our first production as OperaUpClose, and was based at The Cock Tavern Theatre since the company was founded in October 2009 until May 2010, before transferring to Soho Theatre in summer 2010. We are always excited to form new links with venues, and want to bring our unique work to as many new audiences as possible.

'Leading an artistic revolution' **The Sunday Times**

Part of our mission is to bring opera to audiences who ordinarily might avoid it. We aim to make our productions as clear and engaging as possible, working with new English translations, and bringing the narrative to the forefront of our work.

We are also keen to develop our education work. We have begun holding workshops in schools to introduce opera to young people. If you're interested in us holding workshops at your school do please get in touch on the contact details below.

If you'd like to help us continue to make exciting work, or if we can support your corporate, charity or personal event with a magical private performance, please contact Dominic Haddock on 0207 226 8561 or dominic.haddock@kingsheadtheatre.com

'Every word makes sense; every emotion hits you in the pit of the stomach' **Evening Standard**

In October 2010, Adam Spreadbury-Maher became artistic director of the King's Head Theatre in Islington. As the resident company, OperaUpClose has staged new versions of Rossini's *The Barber of Seville* (directed by Robin Norton-Hale) and *Cinderella* (directed by Emma Rivlin), a radical re-imagining of Puccini's *Madame Butterfly* (directed by Adam Spreadbury-Maher), a jazz-inspired version of Monteverdi's *The Coronation of Poppea* (directed by Mark Ravenhill), a chilling new production of Britten's *The Turn of the Screw* (directed by Edward Dick), and *Manifest Destiny*, a new opera by Keith Burstein to mark the 10th anniversary of 9/11.

Future plans for OperaUpClose in 2012 include a new version of Bizet's *Carmen* (directed by Rodula Gaitanou) coming in April, Sir Arnold Wesker and Robert Saxton's rarely-performed opera *Caritas* (directed by Pamela Howard) to celebrate Wesker's 80th birthday in May, and a major new adaptation of Puccini's *Tosca* (directed by Adam Spreadbury-Maher) in the autumn.

Thank you for supporting us by coming to see *La Fanciulla del West (West End Girl)*. We hope to see you in the future for more opera which will be fresh, exciting, challenging, and of course, up close.

Adam Spreadbury-Maher & Robin Norton-Hale
Artistic Directors, OperaUpClose

Executive

Artistic Director	Adam Spreadbury-Maher
Executive Producer	Dominic Haddock
Co-Artistic Director, OperaUpClose	Robin Norton-Hale

Administrative

General Manager	Holly Aston
Theatre Manager	Louisa Davis
Assistant to the Directors /Finance Administrator	Kat Ould

Production

Producer	Rachel Lerman
Press & Marketing Assistant	Thomas Meerstadt

OperaUpClose Associates

Associate Director	Mark Ravenhill
Associate Artist	Toby Scholz

King's Head Theatre Associates

Associate Director	Hamish MacDougall
Associate Artist	Nathan Lang
Associate Artist	Shelley Lang
Associate Artist	Tim O'Hara
Archivist	Carly Donaldson-Randall
Literary Associate	Robyn Winfield-Smith
International Literary Associate	Tanja Pugnaco

COMING SOON

OPERA & THEATRE

SOMEONE TO BLAME
Directed by David Mercatali

In 2004, Sam Hallam aged 17 was convicted of murder during a street fight. But there was no CCTV. No forensics. And he denies he was even there. This new piece of verbatim theatre tells his story.

6 - 31 March

CARMEN
Directed by Rodula Gaitanou

A new version of Bizet's classic opera, where a young woman becomes the fatal link between the lawful society and the underworld where she belongs.

3 April – 5 May

DENIAL
Directed by Adam Spreadbury-Maher

The London premiere of Arnold Wesker's controversial false-memory play comes to the King's Head Theatre for his 80th birthday.

15 May – 9 June

CARITAS
Directed by Pamela Howard

Arnold Wesker and Robert Saxton's opera about a young woman who makes a decision about her life which she can't relinquish.

21 May – 10 June

LA FANCIULLA DEL WEST
(WEST END GIRL)

Puccini's
LA FANCIULLA DEL WEST
(WEST END GIRL)

A new version by Robert Chevara & Kfir Yefet

OBERON BOOKS
LONDON

WWW.OBERONBOOKS.COM

First published in 2012 by Oberon Books Ltd
521 Caledonian Road, London N7 9RH
Tel: +44 (0) 20 7607 3637 / Fax: +44 (0) 20 7607 3629
e-mail: info@oberonbooks.com
www.oberonbooks.com

A catalogue record for this book is available from the British
Library.

ISBN: 978-1-84943-190-3

Cover image by Christopher Tribble

Printed and bound by CPI Group (UK) Ltd, Croydon, CR0 4YY.

For Jörn

Writers' Acknowledgments

Julie Bakewell

Rikki Beadle-Blair

Elinor Burns

Pamela Callaghan

Emma Cattell

Patricia Killaspy

Jonathan Lipman

Bertie Marshall

Brian Smith

Sarah Thom

Characters

MINNIE
A London girl

'VIK' JOHNSON
East European itinerant

JACK ROCK
Albanian petty criminal

SONORA
Montenegrin henchman

YURI
Bosnian labourer

NIK
Russian barman

Act 1

Soho. An internet café – 'Minnie's'. Essentially tacky but trying to be respectable. There's a bar with a few stools in one corner and a couple of computer terminals. There's also a small card-table and chairs, and a TV on the wall.

The place is dark. Something about it suggests simmering violence.

There's only one figure onstage – a young man in labouring clothes, YURI, hunched over one of the computers. He's wearing earphones and singing softly into the computer's microphone.

YURI: Hello! Hello!
               It's Daddy. It's Daddy.
               Hello! Hello!
               Ah…back home. Ah…back home.
               Don't you cry for me.

From behind the counter, the barman, NIK, enters and immediately turns on the cable TV.

JACK ROCK enters. He's an Albanian petty criminal. A tough man in a cheap suit.

ROCK: Evenin'. What's up? What's happening?

NIK: *(Glancing at YURI.)*
               Same old problem. Nostalgia.
               They're thinking about home! Remembering
               what they've left there.
               All the mothers they might never see again…

Discreetly, another young East European labourer, SONORA, enters and goes straight to the card-table.

ROCK: This fucking place! I thought the streets were
               golden.

29

NIK:	We work like dogs! If the work doesn't kill you, the Mafia will.
ROCK:	And Minnie? She's late.
SONORA:	*(To YURI.)* How much you got?
YURI:	*(Joining him at the table.)* Twenty.
SONORA:	And Eighty, makes a Hundred. Jack. Queen…
NIK:	Bullseye! Here we go!

He brings over some drinks and sits down to play too.

YURI:	Fuck's sake!
NIK:	*(An aside about YURI.)* Sarajevan shit face.
NIK:	The three never wins.
SONORA:	*(To spite him.)* All on three!
NIK:	Don't listen. Bye-bye.
NIK:	*(Checking his watch.)* Oh, God – it's starting! Shit, I almost forgot.

He turns the TV channel to Strictly Come Dancing.

SONORA:	Come Dancing? Fuck that. I don't dance with nobody, do I?

He holds out his hand. NIK takes it.

NIK:	You said it.

They start dancing.

SONORA:	Minnie – you think she really wants me?
NIK:	Sure. She said you're the one she prefers.

SONORA: Drinks all round!

MEN: *(Excited.)*
              No way! No way!

NIK tops up everyone's drinks.

*SONORA starts channel-hopping through various foreign TV channels.
Something catches his eye. An ageing East-European folk singer,
ILYA POPOV, is crooning a sentimental ditty they all seem to know.*

ILYA POPOV: *(On TV.)*
              What will they do those old folks of mine?
              All the way back there. All the way there.
              Sad and lonely, on their own,
              Crying their eyes out. Tearing their hearts out.
              'Cos I won't be back.

NIK: *Jesu Christo!* That idiot Ilya Popov.
              How we all love the old songs…

ILYA POPOV: *(On TV.)*
              And my Mama…Where is she?
              Can I find her? Will I find her?
              Does she weep for me?

ALL: Does she weep for me? She's there waiting…

ILYA/MEN 2:   …lined with sorrow…

ILYA/MEN 1:   …getting older, for my return…

ALL: …she's there waiting…

MEN 1:   …lined with sorrow…

MEN 2:   …getting older…
              For my return.

ILYA: My old folks…

SONORA: …How do they look?

ALL: My old folks…

MEN 2:   What will my old folks do?

ILYA/MEN: Thinking I'll never come back again.

ALL: Never again. I want to weep.

ILYA: Thinking…

MEN: No more.

SONORA: Ah!

ILYA: Cos I won't be back!

SONORA: Makes me want to weep.

MEN: Will my mates pretend to know me?
              Will my mates still…

ILYA: Will my mates still…

ALL: Still remember me?
              Ah! Ah!

NIK: Oh, my home that felt so safe…

MEN 1:   Way back home.
              Way back home.

MEN 2:   Way back home.
              Will you remember?
              Oh, my place that felt so safe,
              Way back home.

ILYA/MEN: Home, home, home…

ALL: Back home.

ROCK: Poker? Nik – blinis!

YURI: *(Holding up his cards.)*
              Boss man, let's go.

ROCK: Fellas, meet The Man. Mr Yuri –
              The baddest fucker I know.

YURI: Nik, bring me a beer.
           How the hell is the girl?

NIK: Great, thank you.

ROCK/
SONORA: *(Looking suspiciously at YURI.)*
           Great, thank you.

ROCK: Any news of the villain Ramazov?

YURI: For three months we've searched.
           He's back in Soho.

ROCK: They say he kills just like a Gypsy. Is he
           Romanian?

YURI: The band of dogs he runs with are all Polaks.
           Ferocious, brutal,
           Hungry, ready for badness.
           Keep an eye out, mark my words.
           I'm dead beat, but one of these…
           (He dips a finger in a little sachet and snorts some coke.)
           And now I feel much better!

NIK fills up all their glasses.

NIK: Drinks on Minnie.

ALL: Long live Minnie!
           The lovely Minnie!

ROCK: Mrs Rock, one day…

SONORA: Huh! Careful what you wish for.
           Minnie is not for a slag like you.

ROCK: Shithead! It's the whiskey that's talking.
           You're just gutted.
           But Jack Rock has never, ever –
           Listen – *never* been used like someone's bitch.
           Get it?
           Lucky for you I'm not bothered
           By a drunken twat like you.

SONORA:	The shit's pouring out of you. Minnie don't want you.
ROCK:	Prove it!
SONORA:	*(Getting drunker.)* *You* prove it. Wanker!
ROCK:	Prove it!
SONORA:	The shit's pouring out of you!
ROCK:	Bastard…
SONORA:	Minnie don't want you…
ROCK:	Ah… Bastard…

He suddenly pulls out his gun and fires wildly at SONORA. At that moment, MINNIE enters through the audience, runs onstage and grabs the revolver from ROCK's hand.

ALL:	Hello, Minnie! Hello, Minnie! Hello, Minnie!
MINNIE:	What the fuck's happening? You again, Jack Rock!
NIK:	Listen, Boss. They're joking. They were laughing.
MINNIE:	Yes, laughing at everything I've tried to do here! Shame on you!
NIK:	Minnie…
MINNIE:	That's an end to the lessons.
MEN 1:	No, Minnie!
MEN 2:	No, Minnie!
SONORA:	Sorry, when you're late we get bored… And then…
MINNIE:	*(Tapping YURI's nose)* And then what, Yuri? Then what?

YURI: *(Ashamed.)*
Nothing…

ALL: Nothing at all.

NIK takes out a CD in a clear case and hands it to MINNIE.

NIK: Minnie, I just heard this on Spotify.
I ran straight out to Berwick St and bought it.

MINNIE: *(Cooly.)*
That's very sweet…

SONORA: That crazy junkie came in earlier, the one from
Old Compton St.
Selling one thing and another.
I bought this for you. A present. He said it was
just nicked,
but I thought you might like it.

SONORA gives her a red dress. NIK has bought her a blue one – exactly the same.

NIK: And this one too, from the same bloke!

MINNIE: Cheers, you two.

NIK: I made some money on the dogs.

MINNIE: Sweet talker!
(To Rock)
Hope you're having fun, big guy.

ROCK: Good evening, Minnie.

SONORA: *(Handing MINNIE a wad of cash.)*
Strike a mark through my tab.

MINNIE stashes it away where she stores all the labourers' money – inside a book-safe which she replaces on a shelf behind the bar.

YURI: With all these desperate gangs around
It's stupid to leave our money here like this.
But the fucking banks won't even let us in the
door.

From next to the book-safe, MINNIE takes down the booklet 'Life in the UK – A Journey to Citizenship'. She leafs through the pages.

MINNIE: Yuri, where were we?
Tax? The NHS? No.
Housing? No. Ah, here we go…
'History and Significance of the Royal Family'.
Nik, remember Elizabeth?

The four men start gathering around her.

NIK: She was Queen, Queen of England, the one with red hair.
Who wore a lot of make-up, like armour.
She had an eye for the fellas.
And slaughtered anyone she didn't like.

MINNIE: That's not quite right…
Sit down, Citizen Nikolai.
Let's make a start. Listen and learn.
Elizabeth is married to Prince Philip.

NIK: Did you just say married, Minnie?

MINNIE: Yes this is the current Elizabeth.

NIK: So she'll be our Queen too?

MINNIE: Yes, of course. She's the Queen of *all* her subjects.
Of all the men and women.

NIK: Her subjects?

MINNIE: Her citizens.

(Putting the booklet down and looking into the distance.)

The day my daddy died I cried my eyes out.
I wrote to Tony Blair asking him to adopt me.
And then to Kylie Minogue.
But they never did answer.

So I'll always remember, the only one,
One person, who wrote to me.
Signed – *Her Majesty*.
And that letter is on that wall.
I'd advise every one of you to read it,
And maybe one day you'll get one of your own.

Suddenly, a voice from the computer: 'You've got mail'.

YURI: *(Running to the computer station.)*
           Here it is! A message back from Olga.
           Olga Urbanskaya.

MINNIE: She's that tart from deepest Deptford.
           A native of Kosovo,
           A real princess all caked in make-up and
           drunken giggles.
           They say she's always up for it.
           Ask any of her 'gentlemen'!

Embarrassed, NIK takes a sack of rubbish outside.

YURI: Boss man, tonight that Ramazov is finished.

ROCK: Says who?

YURI: *(Still scanning the email.)*
           His little girlfriend.
           He'll be at her Kosovan whorehouse tonight.
           Banging her at midnight.
           His last midnight.

ROCK: Don't trust Urbanskaya. She's a crack-whore.
           How much we paid her?

YURI: A grand.
           We get our man Ramazov. Right between the
           eyes.
           And her? That mad bitch gets her own back on
           that dog.

NIK: *(To MINNIE.)*

37

There's a stranger… Outside.

MINNIE: A cop?

NIK: No, I don't think so. Looks like an Estonian.
He asked for a whiskey and water!

MINNIE: Whiskey and water?
Is he fucking joking?

NIK: That's what I told him:
At Minnie's we drink our whiskey straight.

MINNIE: What a loser.
Let's see if we can teach him.

NIK leaves. ROCK follows MINNIE to the bar.

ROCK: I love you truly, Minnie.

MINNIE: Not again.

ROCK: A million quid, if you just kiss me.

MINNIE: Rock, don't make me laugh.
Get going. I mean it.

ROCK: You can't stay all alone.
Let's get married!

MINNIE: And your wife? Back at home?

ROCK: Just say the word. I'll make her disappear.

MINNIE: Rock, don't!
Rock, don't insult me.
Living alone like this, you well know,
Really does suit me.

(She reaches under the bar and pulls out a small hand-pistol.)

With this little baby I'm never alone.
He never lets me down.
Rock, just leave me in peace.

(ROCK goes grimly towards the card table.)

You still don't get it, Rock? But why?
Can't we just be honest with each other?

ROCK:　　Minnie, when I left my little house,
Right up in the mountains, beside the Baltic sea.
No one cried, Minnie. Who gave a shit?
No one wept. No one loved me. No one cared.
Nothing ever gave me any real pleasure.
Deep inside is the heart of a monster,
Brutal, broken in pieces.
Waiting for a miracle to happen.
All I wanted when I came here –
The power you can only buy with gold.
That's all I've had to keep my dream alive.
But now I see –
The dream is you!

MINNIE:　　Love is another thing…

ROCK:　　How poetic!

MINNIE:　　Way back when I was small, we lived in Stratford.
Daddy ran a dirty, stinking, little fish-and-chip shop.
I'd go and help him out, when I got back from school,
With my sweet little mother.
Ah, so many memories.
Seeing people eating, laughing, shouting.
Mother served both food and drinks,
Daddy fried and pickled, pickled and fried.
Mum was kind of pretty, she had an inner joy.
She'd sing and dance when she felt low.
And me – I'd sit and watch them,
See them hold each other,

39

Like magnets, they couldn't quite keep apart.
Until the day she died, every moment counted,
Every kiss lasted forever.
Oh – so much beauty! Oh – so much love!
Now, I search to find that kind of love.

ROCK: Maybe that man is with you right now?

NIK comes back in. A young man is following behind him. He looks at MINNIE intently.

JOHNSON: So you're the one who's gonna teach me?

MINNIE stares back at him. All other movement in the room has stopped.

MINNIE: You bet your life I will.

JOHNSON: And you'll do that with whiskey and water?

MINNIE: I could do…
Nik, get him a whiskey, he must be thirsty.
With water, if he insists…

JOHNSON: You look like the owner.

MINNIE: Do I?

ROCK: We don't get strangers. Except when there's trouble.
And you've got trouble written all over you.
Maybe you've got a date with Olga Urbanskaya?

MINNIE: Rock!

JOHNSON: I heard I could write private messages here.
With no one snooping.
And if by any chance, you run a game…

ROCK: A game! And who might you be?

MINNIE: Since when have we ever asked anyone's name?

JOHNSON: Johnson.

ROCK: *Johnson.* What else?

JOHNSON: Born in Sarajevo.

MINNIE: We're happy to meet you, Johnson from
           Sarajevo.

JOHNSON: Thank you.

(Whispering to MINNIE.)

           Do you really remember?

MINNIE: Yes. If you also remember…

JOHNSON: And how could I not? You stood me up.
           I waited at Notting Hill.

MINNIE: You didn't wait.
           You sent one text which I deleted…

JOHNSON: At least I sent it. I suggested a latte with sugar.

MINNIE: But I drink tea…

JOHNSON: Oh, really?

MINNIE: I actually told you.

JOHNSON: We only met once…

MINNIE: You said you'd remember.
           You promised to.
           Or did you forget that too…?

JOHNSON: No, of course I remember.
           I said that from that second…

MINNIE: That you'd never forget me.

JOHNSON: And I've never forgotten you…you…you…

MINNIE: How I hoped you'd take the Central line again.
           But you never did.

ROCK: Mister Johnson,
You get on my tits.
I'm Jack Rock. The Boss Man.
Don't you ever forget that.
What do you really want?

(No answer.)

Fellas, some bloody stranger refuses to say
What he wants in our cafe.

MEN: What's that? What's that?
He'd better start singing. He'd better start
dancing.

MINNIE: I swear I know him!
Before every one of you,
I'll stand up for Johnson.

SONORA: Nice to meet you, Mr Johnson.

JOHNSON: Delighted. Good evening.

NIK: *(Pointing at ROCK behind his back)*
I can't help laughing at him.
That fucking bully really got what he deserved
for once!

MINNIE: *(Spoken.)*
NIK!

NIK: *(As HARRY.)*
Mr Johnson – do you waltz?

JOHNSON: With pleasure.
(To MINNIE.)
Will you join me?

MINNIE: What…? Forgive me. I know you won't believe
this,
But I've never danced in public.

JOHNSON: Let's go.

ALL: Go, Minnie.

MINNIE: *(To MEN.)*
            OK, I will then.

MEN: *Musica!*
            Hip, hip, hooray *(Etc.)*

The MEN start humming and clapping an accompaniment as MINNIE and JOHNSON start to dance, tentatively at first, then growing more intimate. Discreetly, the MEN leave the Café as MINNIE and JOHNSON dance slowly and intensely at the front of the stage.

MINNIE: Mister Johnson,
            Have you really stayed only to keep
            me company,
            And to guard my takings?

JOHNSON: I did and I didn't.
            The weirdest thing! Finding you right here
            Among these dealers and chancers…
            Oh, and killers.
            That's the weirdest thing – finding you right
            here!

MINNIE: Take me at my word.
            I can really look after myself…

JOHNSON: Even when a bloke only wants to steal
            A kiss?

MINNIE: Especially then. I've had a couple of near misses.
            But with my very first kiss I must be sure,
            Totally sure in my heart.

JOHNSON: If that's true, you're right to be so careful.

MINNIE: I live way up at the top of a tower block.

JOHNSON: You deserve so much better.

MINNIE: I really love it.
            It's all I need, believe me.
            I live all alone.
            Alone, not lonely.
            I feel like I can really trust you,
            Though I don't know you,
            Not the first thing about you.

JOHNSON: I'm not so sure who I am either.
            I've always loved life, and it's so beautiful to me.
            I'm sure you love it too.
            But you haven't seen enough to guard against
            the rotten,
            Stinking shit of this world…

MINNIE: How wrong you are.
            I'm a very working-class girl,
            A grafter and a dreamer.
            I'm not a slag or a slapper.
            I think you know that.
            Some people judge me harshly.
            They don't know me.
            My soul, it longs for something,
            I don't know how to explain it.
            It's a feeling I can be myself with you.
            You. You. You. Your light is shining.
            Just being so near you
            Just feeling so close to you.

JOHNSON: What you can't say now from your broken heart,
            When I held you I already knew,
            While dancing with me,
            Pulling you close to me – in bliss.
            Suddenly, a joy so strange.
            The first peace I've known,
            I have ever felt.

MINNIE: Why do the words come so easily to you?
But my body tingles with such emotion,
With such fear…

The MEN *start reappearing.*

MINNIE: *(To NIK.)*
What's the matter?

NIK: Watch out.
There's another dirty Bosnian out there, lurking.

MINNIE: No way, Nik.

JOHNSON: Don't go out there.

(He gets a text alert on his mobile.)

(To himself.)
Shit, the signal.

MINNIE: What the hell?
Who's texting you now?
In this room, Johnson, there's a treasure.
All the dreams of those boys out there.

JOHNSON: And they leave them here?

MINNIE: Every night without fail
One or two take turns to guard the moula.
It's unfair, they can't open bank accounts or get credit.
Oh, they're accused of just about everything,
even money laundering!
They deserve better.
Poor boys. How many are there
Who left a family at home,
A wife, their kids,
And work here, treated like pigs,
In jobs where they're invisible,
They're exploited and used.

I try to help,
to give them a little hope.
Johnson – see why anyone who took their money
Answers to me.

JOHNSON: Oh don't you fear,
no one would dare!
How I love to hear those brave words!
But I must disappear.
I'd have loved to come and say a last goodbye.
In your little flat…

MINNIE: Well then why don't you? I mean it.
The boys will be back in just a few minutes.
When they're here, I'll go home.
If you want to continue our chat,
We'll get to know each other
Better in private.

JOHNSON: I'm with you, Minnie. Sweet.

MINNIE: Don't expect too much!
I'm not some Chav,
but I'm also not educated.
Well not in the usual way.
But I get by.
I always will.

JOHNSON: We could both be something.
I'm beginning to really see you, oh, Minnie.

MINNIE: The real me? Are you sure?

(She burst into tears.)

I'm no one and you know it.

JOHNSON: Don't, Minnie. Please don't cry…
You don't know what you're worth.

Don't grow old here.
You're a beautiful free spirit,
And you have the face of an angel.

He stares at her for another moment, then quickly runs out.

MINNIE: What was that…? What was it he said?
The face of an angel…

The lights slowly start to dim. Minnie stands there, totally still, illuminated in silhouette by the silver glow of the computer screens, until they too snap out – to **Blackout**.

Act 2

A dark, empty little bedroom. We're in a council flat on the 30ᵗʰ floor of a tower block in Stratford, East London. Through the window, the cranes of the nearby Olympic Park glitter in the night sky.

MINNIE enters in a rush and turns on the overhead light. It becomes apparent that this is her room, but it seems more like the fossilized bedroom of a ten-year-old girl: a bunk-bed in a corner, a mini-desk and chair by the window and a small pink wardrobe. A tattered poster of Minnie Mouse is pinned to the wall. It's obviously been there for some years.

MINNIE runs straight to the wardrobe and throws it open. She pulls out a pair of ridiculously high-heeled stilettos.

MINNIE: These should do it, I think.
            These little beauties from Top Shop.
            If only I could just – get them on me!
            Ouch, they're killing me. God, that's tight…

(In the mirror.)

            Look at you. Look at you. Really think he's
            gonna like you?
            I'm gonna pull all the stops out,
            Like those girls on the catwalks.
            I'm gonna show him I got it.
            No, I ain't such a loser.
            A drop of perfume. There.
            And these earrings. It's been years since I've
            worn them.
            Or are they just a bit too much?

JOHNSON: *(From outside.)*
            Hello? Hello? HELLO?

MINNIE: Oh, shit. Too late now.

VIK JOHNSON enters the room.

JOHNSON: Hello!

MINNIE: You let yourself in?

JOHNSON: It was open…

MINNIE: Yes… No… Dunno. Come in, then.

He looks around the room, noticing the Minnie Mouse poster.

JOHNSON: Now I see why they call you…
              I'm sorry. I didn't mean to offend you.

MINNIE: Why should I be offended?
              You keep getting it wrong.

JOHNSON: It's just… You look so fucking gorgeous.

MINNIE: That's a new one on me but thank you.

JOHNSON: God, now *I'm* embarrassed.

MINNIE: Embarrassed or sorry?

JOHNSON: Both.

(He suddenly sits at her desk)

              I'm staying.
              I knew it. We're soulmates. I know what you're
              thinking.

MINNIE: That's more than I do.
              Tonight at the Café – you didn't come there for
              me.
              What brought you in there, I wonder.
              Maybe it's true, you mistook me for someone…
              Just like Urbanskaya!

(JOHNSON gets up.)

              Hold it right there.

JOHNSON: I'm just looking around.

MINNIE: Looking is free…

49

JOHNSON: *(Looking through everything – a little puzzled.)*
I'm surrounded by pieces of you.
How strange, your little life, so high up here,
Looking down on the world.

MINNIE: If you only knew what a good life I have here.
I've got a little motorbike that I ride in summer.

(Pointing out of the window.)

I love to get out to Essex, the little country pubs,
The little country clubs, the all-night raves,
Vodka and the beer flow as long as you want them.
Then I start making my way back through Epping Forest,
I feel so high I can almost feel my Daddy reaching down to me from heaven and stroking my hair.
For a moment there's no one else, just him and me.
I feel so beautiful and so free that I tell you,
Sometimes I just wanna take his hand and say:
'*Take me away!*'

JOHNSON: And when the summer's over?

MINNIE: Oh, well… Then I'm busy.
That's when the Café opens.

JOHNSON: The internet place?

MINNIE: Well it's kind of a 'school' for workers.

JOHNSON: And who's the teacher?

MINNIE: Pleased to meet you.

(Going to the door)

Can I get you a Pepsi?

JOHNSON: Thank you… So you like reading?

MINNIE: All day.

JOHNSON: I'll send you my blog.

MINNIE: Great… But don't leave anything out.

JOHNSON: OK, I won't. Are you sure?

MINNIE: Yes. Be honest. For me, it's everything. Honesty
is everything.
I'll never understand, what is it with you guys?
You can really chase a girl,
And then you dump her.
After less than an hour…

JOHNSON: You couldn't be more mistaken.
One hour spent with a certain kind of girl…
Well, a certain kind of guy, he'd quite happily
Make that hour – his last one!

MINNIE: Oh, really? And how many last hours have you
had?

(Going to the window.)

Wanna see the view? It's awesome.

(JOHNSON comes up behind her and kisses her neck.)

Mind – my little earrings. You'll eat them!

JOHNSON: Here, let me take them off.

(Holding her tightly from behind.)

You need me. You get me. I know you get me.

MINNIE: Mister Johnson. Oh, I get you alright. You think
I'm easy.

JOHNSON: You're so mistaken. Where my heart goes, I
follow.

MINNIE: Look, if you just wanna crash, an hour, two at most…

JOHNSON: If I crash, I crash with you!

MINNIE: *(Taking a deep breath.)*
You said it. Get ready. *Crash!*

They kiss passionately, just in front of the window. As their lips touch, the harsh ceiling light trips out and slowly the soft, mysterious pink and red table-lamps around the room start fading up.

JOHNSON: Minnie – the sweetest name.

MINNIE: You like it?

JOHNSON: I love it. Right back when I first saw you…

(Stopping himself.)

No, don't look at me. Don't listen to my bullshit, Minnie.
It's pie in the sky.

MINNIE: Why do you talk bullshit?
I know I'm not all that. I get it.
From the first time you walked in I said to myself:
Oh, God. I like him. No, not just like.
If I'm honest, I'm *mad* about him.

JOHNSON: Take care of yourself. I'll see you.

(He opens the door, then stops himself.)

What time is it?

MINNIE: *(Pointing out of the window.)*
Look, the last tube has gone.
No way can you get home now.

JOHNSON: I have to.

MINNIE: But why? Tomorrow, they start again at five.

It's cool. Just stay.

Distant gunshots are heard.

JOHNSON: What the fuck?

MINNIE: Nothing. Maybe gangs, maybe Ramazov.
           What do we care?

JOHNSON: What do we care…?

MINNIE: Stay. I really want you to.

JOHNSON: OK. But I just wanna say –

(He holds her face in his hands.)

           I'll never let you go –
           I'll never let you go –
           From now it's me and you until the end.
           Hand in hand, side by side, me and you.

JOHNSON
& MINNIE: So I'll never let you go –
           I'll never let you go –
           I've waited so long and here you are.

MINNIE: Make me believe it – whatever you want.

JOHNSON: Whatever I want – you'll want it too?

MINNIE: I'll want whatever you want, I swear.

JOHNSON: Oh, believe me, you will.
           And then you'll be mine –

JOHNSON
& MINNIE: Forever!
           The ecstasy goes on and on.
           Forever and ever,
           Just when I thought it was gone.
           I only *thought* I was living,
           Just living day-to-day.

But that was death!
Until the day I met you.

MINNIE slowly goes to stare out of the window.

JOHNSON: Minnie, you OK?

MINNIE: I was dreaming. That was just so cool,
Now it's almost time for nighty-night.

(Pointing to the bunk-bed.)

You go up there. I'll take the one below.

JOHNSON: You're joking, right?

MINNIE: I'd rather, just for tonight.
It's all been so perfect,
I really don't wanna spoil it.
I'll wrap myself up in Daddy's sheepskin coat,
And fall asleep.

One by one she switches off the floor lamps around the room. She starts to undress shyly. JOHNSON does the same and they get into their separate beds.

MINNIE: Tell me one more thing.
Something to make me dream.

JOHNSON: Just... I love you.

MINNIE smiles and curls up under the sheepskin coat.

Silence. JOHNSON slowly climbs out of bed and goes to listen at the door.

JOHNSON: What was that?

MINNIE: This whole tower's falling down.

JOHNSON: Sounds like people whispering.

MINNIE: I swear it's just the building.

(JOHNSON goes on looking out of the window suspiciously. MINNIE gazes at him)

What's your real name?

JOHNSON:	Viktor.

MINNIE: For real? Vik?

JOHNSON: For real.

MINNIE: And you've really never met Olga Urbanskaya?

JOHNSON: No.

MINNIE: Sweet dreams.

JOHNSON: *(Still at the window.)*
Sweet dreams.

From outside, a noise.

NIK: *(Whispering.)*
Hello… In here…

MINNIE: Now I hear it.

JOHNSON: *(Grabbing something from his jacket.)*
Don't say a word. Zip it!

MINNIE: Don't let him hear you. He's crazy, Jack Rock.

NIK: *(Outside)*
Hey, hey!
They've seen Ramazov breaking into her flat.

MINNIE: Shit, they've come to help me…

She grabs JOHNSON and quickly bundles him into her wardrobe. Just as she shuts the door, JACK ROCK, NICK, YURI and SONORA burst into the room.

SONORA: It's OK! We've got you!

NIK: We've been watching a couple of hours.

MINNIE: But what the fuck?

ROCK: We were frightened for you.

MINNIE: For me?

YURI: Your darling Johnson…

NIK: The Polak.

ROCK: Your dancing partner – he was Ramazov!

MINNIE: That's bullshit. All bullshit. Pure bullshit.

ROCK: Turns out that your perfect little *'Mr Johnson from Sarajevo'*,
            Is a Polak drug-runner!

MINNIE: *(More and more upset.)*
            Shit. This is shit.
            For sure – a load of bull!

ROCK: Watch it. If you're as big a mug again the next time…

MINNIE: Do I look like a mug? No. *You're* the mug.

YURI: Tonight at the Café – he was there to steal.

MINNIE: But he did no such thing.

SONORA: No, that's true. He didn't steal.
            But he easily could have.

ROCK: He was seen on his bike, heading east,
            Burning up the road to Stratford.
            Is that right, Nik?

NIK: That's right.

ROCK: And the trail ended here.
            But you haven't seen him.
            So where could he be?

They look around the room. NIK spots JOHNSON's watch on the bedside table.

NIK: *(To himself.)*
     That fucking watch of his. He's here.

(To the others, trying to help MINNIE.)

     Maybe we were mistaken.
     They're all a bunch of liars.

MINNIE: But who's the one who first said it?
     That the villain was Johnson?

ROCK: His bitch.

MINNIE: His bitch? Who?

ROCK: Olga.

MINNIE: Olga Urbanskaya? *He knows her?*

ROCK: He loves her.
     When we realized he'd screwed us over,
     We picked up that other Polak, Krizstof.
     And we dragged him to that whorehouse – *'The Palms'.*
     Turns out we were expected.
     Olga was there. She pulled out her mobile and there was this picture –

(Showing her a photo on a mobile phone.)

     Familiar?

MINNIE inspects the picture, then starts laughing hysterically.

ROCK: What's so funny?

MINNIE: *(Towards the wardrobe.)*
     Oh, nothing, fuck all. Just the company he keeps.
     Such special people. *Olga!*

SONORA:	You got it.
MINNIE:	OK, boys. The show's over. Get out.
SONORA:	We'll get out of your hair.
MINNIE:	I'd appreciate that.
YURI:	Let's split.
NIK:	*(To MINNIE.)* Just give me the word…
MINNIE:	The word is no.
YURI:	Good night.

They all leave.

MINNIE slowly goes to the wardrobe and stares at the closed door.

MINNIE:	Heard enough? Heard enough? HEARD ENOUGH? So you came here to rob me!
JOHNSON:	*(Bursting out.)* No!
MINNIE:	You're lying!
JOHNSON:	No!
MINNIE:	Yes!
JOHNSON:	That's what they're saying, but –
MINNIE:	Oh, fuck you! Why come here, if not to rob me?
JOHNSON:	Because the day I saw you –
MINNIE:	Forget it! Forget it! Don't move an inch. I'll call the coppers. A dealer! A fucking assassin! Ah, ah… I sure can pick 'em. A liar! A liar! Now get the fuck out. Out, out, *OUT!*
JOHNSON:	Just one final word.

I won't try to change your mind.

Yes, I'm a villain. It's true. It's true!

But I'd never have robbed from you.

I am Ramazov. Yes, I was born in Poland.

The whole family were criminals,

But did I know it? No.

As long as my dad was alive I didn't have a clue.

Six months ago, my father was killed.

All I could do to support them – my mother, my brothers,

Was take up the offer – the only thing my father left me:

A position in a gang of traffickers.

What could I do?

No other way to stay alive.

But then one day, I met you.

I fooled myself that one day we'd be together.

So far away.

And redeeming my life, by working and living,

Just by living with you.

And in my heart,

A murmuring, stuttering prayer – Oh, God –

May she never know anything,

Never know of my shame!

Oh, shame on me. Shame on me.

The dream was all in vain.

Wake up. It's all over.

MINNIE: Listen, so you're a killer.

You can ask God's forgiveness.

But that first kiss that I gave you,

The kiss you asked for –

I'll never get it back. As long as I live.

Get out. Get out.

They're gonna kill you! What do I care?

JOHNSON: *(Leaving quietly.)*
             I'll seeya.

Silence. He's gone.

MINNIE: Now it's over. All over.

             (A shot is heard. She stops herself)

             They've shot him. What do I care?

She waits another moment, then rushes out and drags JOHNSON's wounded body back into the room.

JOHNSON: What the hell are you doing?
             I can't stay here. *No!*

MINNIE: *Shut it!*

JOHNSON: No!

MINNIE: *Shut it!*

JOHNSON: You're out your fucking mind! Let me go!

MINNIE: Shut it!

JOHNSON: *No!*

MINNIE: Shut it!

JOHNSON: *No!*

MINNIE: For God's sake, you're wounded. I'm hiding you
             here.

JOHNSON: *No!*

MINNIE: You're wounded! Hide yourself... Hide
             yourself...

JOHNSON: Open the door – I have to get out!

MINNIE: Stay here!

JOHNSON: *No!*

MINNIE: Stay here!

JOHNSON: *No!*

MINNIE: Stay here!

JOHNSON: *No!*

MINNIE: I love you…
            Stay here! Stay here!
            Ah!
            You, the first man that I ever let come near me!
            You cannot die!

She starts pushing him up the steps to the upper bunk bed with great difficulty.

MINNIE: Up, up, up – quickly…

JOHNSON: No…

MINNIE: Up! Save yourself!

JOHNSON: I'm losing strength…

MINNIE: Up, up, up – save yourself.
            Then – we'll go – away – together.

They're almost at the top.

JOHNSON: I'm – lo – sing – strength…

MINNIE: You're not. You're fine. You'll do it. You have to.
            I love you. I love you.
            Up! Up!

He collapses onto the upper bunk and MINNIE quickly covers him with blankets and pillows.

A knock on the door. MINNIE climbs down and checks herself in the mirror, then slowly goes to open it. JACK ROCK enters, alone.

MINNIE: What is it this time, Jack?

ROCK: I'm not Jack. I'm the man who'll capture

	That murdering psycho you're hiding.
	I followed him in here – right in this room!
	And now?
MINNIE:	Now, I'm going to bed. You've tired me out with Ramazov!
ROCK:	*(Pointing a gun at the wardrobe.)*
	In there?

(He looks inside.)

	Not here…
	I'm certain I shot him, for sure, I must have.
	He couldn't have got far.
	He has to be here.
MINNIE:	Search if you want. Start looking.
	Start searching wherever you want to.
	And then get out my life for good –
	Once and fucking *forever!*
ROCK:	You swear that he's not here?
MINNIE:	Just carry on what you're doing.
ROCK:	Well, that's that. I've been mistaken.
	But tell me you don't love him.
	Just tell me you don't love him.
MINNIE:	You're crazy!
ROCK:	You got it. I'm crazy for you.
	I love you.
MINNIE:	You coward!
ROCK:	I want you…

He grabs her. They tussle and fall onto the bottom bunk-bed.

MINNIE:	You coward!
	Go! Get out of my bed! You coward!

Get off, get out of my sight, you coward,
Get out!
Ah!

MINNIE manages to free herself. ROCK stays on the bed.

ROCK: What passion! You love him.
Keep yourself for him.
Fine. I'm going. But I swear to you –
He'll never win!

(He starts to get up.)

Shit, what's that?
A drop… A drop of blood.

MINNIE: Maybe I managed to scratch you…

ROCK: No, you didn't scratch me. Look…
The blood keeps coming!

(Staring up at the bunk above his head.)

He's there! He's there!

MINNIE: Oh, God! I'll never let you!

ROCK: Hands off me!

MINNIE: God – *no, no no!* I won't let you! I won't let you!

ROCK: Hands off me…

MINNIE: *No!*

ROCK: Hands off me…

MINNIE: *No! No! No!*

ROCK: *(Standing at the foot of the bed, pointing his gun.)*
Mister Johnson. Come down.

MINNIE: Just wait, just wait.
He can't, he can't.
Believe me, he can't. No.

ROCK: Come down, or God help me…

MINNIE: Hold your horses, Rock. For just a moment
longer.

ROCK: Another moment? But why?
What a turn up!
Would you still like to play a hand with me?
'The Man from Sarajevo'!
The choice is yours – the bullet or the knife?

MINNIE: That's enough, you piece of shit.
Just take a look – he's fainted.
He can't hear a word you're saying.
Let's make a deal between us – and then it's
finished.
What kind of man are you, Jack Rock?
A drugs-runner.
Vik Johnson? Just a dealer.
And me? I run a two-bit café and a bar.
I live by whisky and shots.
Birds of a feather!
All of us cheats and liars!
Tonight you asked me to respond – to your
bitter obsession.
Well here at last is my answer.

ROCK: Thank Christ. What is it?

MINNIE: Here's the big prize if you want it,
Both me and Johnson.
Let's play a hand of poker.
If you win, you take us both,
This dying halfwit and me.
But if I win – swear it first, Jack Rock!
He becomes all mine.
Mine – all mine!

64

ROCK: How you love him! How you love him!
           Alright, you're on! I'll win. I'll win.

MINNIE: First you swear it.

ROCK: I'm a gentleman, even in losing.
           But my God – I'm burning like a flame for you.
           Burning like a witch.
           And if I win – you're mine.

MINNIE: Alright, let's get ready.

As ROCK sits down, MINNIE rummages in a drawer, slipping something into her pocket.

ROCK: Get on with it.

MINNIE: I'd like to use a new pack.
           God, I'm nervous.
           Be patient…
           It's a terrible thing,
           That a simple game of poker,
           Decides a person's fate.
           Are you ready?

ROCK: I'm ready. Cut them. You first.

MINNIE: Here you go. Two out of three.

ROCK: How many?

MINNIE: Two…

ROCK: What is it that makes you love him?

MINNIE: What is it you love in me?

(Pointing at the cards.)

           What you holding?

ROCK: The King.

MINNIE: The King…

ROCK: The Knave.

MINNIE: The Queen…

ROCK: Your game. On to the next hand.

MINNIE: How many?

ROCK: One.

MINNIE: Two.

ROCK: Two Aces and a pair.

MINNIE: Nothing.

ROCK: Equal. We're equal. Come on!

MINNIE: The next one's the decider?

ROCK: Yes. Cut them.

MINNIE: *(Nervously.)*
               Rock… I'm sorry… For saying you were bitter.

ROCK: Play it.

MINNIE :   *(Still clutching her cards.)*
               I've always thought that you were a decent man,
               Jack Rock.
               And I always will.

ROCK: All I really think about is you,
               Pushed against my lips.

   (Plays his cards.)

               Look… Three Kings! *I've done it!*

MINNIE: *(About to faint.)*
               Hold it, Jack. I need help!
               Get me something… I'm losing it.

ROCK: What shall I get you?

MINNIE: *(Pointing to the bedside table behind him.)*

66

There…

ROCK: Ah…the bottle. Over there.
         But where's the bloody glass?

MINNIE quickly pulls something out of her pocket while his back is turned.

MINNIE: Just get it, Jack! I beg you, get it, quick!

ROCK: *(Hands her the bottle and sits opposite.)*
         I know why you fainted.
         You know the game's over.

MINNIE: You're mistaken. I was joyful.
         It's *you* who's finished.

(She slowly reveals her cards.)

    Three Aces and a pair!

Horrified, ROCK gets up from the table. He's in shock.

ROCK: Good night.

He storms out, ripping the Minnie Mouse poster off the wall as he leaves.

MINNIE, laughing hysterically, slowly starts climbing up to the upper bunk.

MINNIE: It's over. He's mine.
         All over.
         He's mine.
         Mine!
         All mine!

She reaches the top, stares down at JOHNSON for another moment, then loses consciousness and collapses onto the bed.

Blackout.

Act 3

A disused underground car park near the Elephant and Castle. Shafts of harsh strip-lighting shine down into the dark recesses. It's a place for drug deals and contract killings. A sense of menace hangs thick in the freezing air.

NIK and JACK ROCK are lurking in the shadows.

NIK: I swear it, Boss Man.
I'd give all my tips from the last five years,
to turn the clock back to a time
before that bastard Johnson, son-of-a-bitch,
somehow got past us and stole her!

ROCK: Twisted wanker.
I was certain he'd died.
And to think all this time,
While we've been freezing our balls off,
He's been there, warmed by Minnie's breath,
Minnie's hands, Minnie's lips…

NIK: Don't, Rock!

ROCK: A nothing from the gutter. I should have told her from the start.

NIK: But you just couldn't do it. You behaved like a real gentleman should.

ROCK: Yeah, right! But what does she see, tell me,
our precious little Minnie,
In that lowlife?

NIK: But what if it's for real? Oh, Love. Oh, Love.
Paradise and Hell, that's all.
All the fucking world's in love.
Maybe for Minnie – now it's her turn to love.

ROCK: Johnson, you fucking Polak,
The devil's helping you!

> But, by God, when I get my hands on you,
> If I don't burn your eyes out,
> If I don't break your fingers,
> Then you can spit in my face!

SONORA and YURI enter, dragging VIK JOHNSON, tied up and hooded, behind them.

ROCK: I knew it!

SONORA: I got him. Jesus! He was like a wolf surrounded by dogs.
           It's not his lucky day.

NIK/
SONORA/
YURI: You fucking immigrant!

ROCK: *Minnie…Minnie… It's all over!*

YURI: Who's got the acid?

SONORA: Who's got the fags?

NIK: We could just cut his balls off?

ALL: Boy, you're gonna dance!

ROCK: *(To himself.)*
           But what do I do? I gave her my word…
           She won his freedom, fair and square…

MEN: And when we see him dance…
           Bang! Bang!
           Can't wait to see him waltzing… Bang! Bang!

ROCK: What did it get you? What did it get you now?

MEN: Dooda-dooda-day!

ROCK: Your pretty…

MEN: Dooda-dooda-day…

ROCK: …boyfriend…

69

Sliced up into bits…

MEN: Dooda…

ROCK: …like dog-food.

MEN: And when we see him dance…
Bang! Bang!
Can't wait to see him waltzing…
Bang! Bang!…

NIK: This is just…
…for you! Enjoy it…

MEN: Hooray, hooray!

NIK: Get that shit ready… Don't let me down.
On my mother's life, believe me, I'll do you.

MEN: Kill him! Kill him! Let's do it!
Let's cut the Polak!

YURI: Boss man, Rock. I give to you this stupid shit, to
hand to our community.
Now he faces justice.

ALL: Yes, he will!

YURI: Good luck. I pray you go to hell.

ROCK removes JOHNSON's gag.

ROCK: And now, Mr Johnson, are you ready?
Anything to say?

JOHNSON: Just get it over quickly!

ROCK: Oh, you'll be in hell in just a minute.

JOHNSON: That's where we both belong.

ROCK: In that case I'll see you there, then.

MEN: Kill him! Kill him! Kill him!

ROCK: Don't you worry, pretty boy.
            It really is nothing.

JOHNSON: Spare me the bullshit… As for dying,
            I don't give a fuck, and you bloody well know it!
            Revolver or knife, who cares!
            Just release one of my hands – I'll slit my own
            throat!
            But I'll tell you something else,
            Of the woman I love.

ROCK: You've got two more minutes to love her.

NIK: Why hang around? Let's do him in now!

YURI: What a performance. He's better off dead.
            Enough! Enough!

NIK: String him up.

YURI: Get the rope.

NIK: Strip him naked.

YURI: Stuff his mouth.

NIK: He'll dance soon enough!

YURI: He'll dance soon enough!

SONORA: Allow him to speak. It's his last rites.

JOHNSON: I thank you, Sonora.
            (Addressing the men.)
            For her, and her alone,
            Who you all love,
            I ask a favour and a promise.
            Never let her know just how I died!

ROCK: Sixty seconds. Be brief.

JOHNSON: Let her believe I'm free and far away,
            Joyfully living a life of happiness!
            Waiting for my return,
            The endless days will drag,

The endless days will drag.
And I will not return…
Will not return.
Minnie, whose love made me pure and made
me better.
Minnie, in my stupid life… My only love.
Ah! You were the only good thing in my life!

ROCK: Very moving. Anything else to say?

JOHNSON: Nothing. Just do it.

They prepare to kill him – Gangland style.

MINNIE is heard offstage.

MINNIE: *Ah, Ah, Ah…*

From nowhere, she appears on a motorbike. She has a gun.

MEN: It's Minnie! It's Minnie! It's Minnie!

ROCK: Just finish him off!
            (No one's listening to him. All eyes are on Minnie.)
            Finish him off! Finish him, finish him off!

MINNIE: No, way! You wouldn't dare!

ROCK: It's only justice.

MINNIE: What kind of justice is this?
            Your word of honour!

ROCK: Careful, girl. Or you'll get it too.

MINNIE: What'll you do? I'm not afraid. Ah…

She points the gun at his head. The men stare at her, stunned.

ROCK: For fuck's sake hold her back. Does none of you
            have any balls?
            A slut waving her gun around!
            Drag her out of here. And quick!

MINNIE brandishes the gun again.

MINNIE: Come on, then!

ROCK: Do it! There will be justice done!

MINNIE: Try it!

MEN: Just kill him.

ROCK: Whore!

MEN: Just kill him. Enough! Enough!

MINNIE: Leave me, or I will kill him, and myself too!

SONORA: Let her go. Let her go. Let her go!

MINNIE: Not one of you ever said 'Enough', when I gave
all my best years for you…
Always there, during your deals and your fights,
I shared your tears and your troubles, I gave you
my youth…
None of you ever said 'Enough'!
Now this man is mine, here, before God!
He's changed beyond all recognition!
He's just trying to get away, trying to start again.
The monster that he was has already died, back
in my flat.
So you cannot kill him again. No!

SONORA: No, Minnie. He wanted more than money…
He took your heart.

MINNIE: My sweet and loyal Sonora, always the first to
forgive.

SONORA: Minnie…

MINNIE: You'll forgive him…
Like you will all forgive him.

MEN: No. Not possible.

MINNIE: You can if you want to.
And you do want to, I know.
Yuri, didn't I find you those flowers,

Like the ones from your homeland?
And Nik – you have to remember,
Lying in bed, delirious, helpless and mad.
You spoke to your dead sister, Lara,
The one you adored.
As I sat with you, night after night.

SONORA: We have to…We owe her too much.

MINNIE: And you, Sonora, whose hand I
guided when….

SONORA: We have to…

MINNIE: …you wrote…

YURI: Not possible.

MINNIE: …those…

MEN: Not possible!

MINNIE: ..first scrawled…

SONORA: Please don't!

MEN: Not possible!

MINNIE: …letters…

SONORA: But she's earned it!

MINNIE: …in English…

SONORA: We've got to!

MINNIE: …to…

MEN: Oh fuck, what can we say?

MINNIE: …Montenegro…

MEN: Not possible.

SONORA: *(To ROCK.)*
You don't own us here!

MINNIE: And you, good…
            …fellas….

SONORA: We can say what goes!

MINNIE: With your eyes…

SONORA: Let go!

ROCK: Not possible.

SONORA: No, we have to listen…

MINNIE: …With your lovely eyes…

SONORA: Come on, fellas!

MEN: No! No!

MINNIE: ..so like a child's…

MEN: We're not mugs.

SONORA: We should do…

MEN: No. It's impossible.

SONORA: …everything to help her.

MINNIE: And all of you, like brothers to me…

MEN: Go against Rock! Not possible.

MINNIE: …in my heart…

SONORA: Decide for yourselves!

MEN: We'd be mugs!

MINNIE: … all such good boys…

MEN 1:   No. It's impossible!

MEN 2:   We'd be mugs!

SONORA: Let's do it!

MEN 1:   Do you want…

MEN 2:   Do you want….

MINNIE: Look, here's…

MEN: It's impossible. No. No.

MINNIE: My revolver.

MEN 1:   We can't refuse you!

MEN 2:   They'd laugh at us.

MINNIE: Look at me…

MEN: We cannot! We cannot!

MINNIE: …I am…

SONORA: All of you, come on!

MINNIE: …still…

SONORA: And you!

MEN: Impossible.

MINNIE: …Your friend…

NIK: She's made me cry!

SONORA: For me. Just do it.

MEN: No. No.

MINNIE: …Your sister…

YURI: Now I'm crying. She's seen me weep!

MEN: Impossible. Impossible.

SONORA: She loves him so much!

MINNIE: …who one day…

MEN: She's such a beauty.

MINNIE: …taught you…

MEN 1:   We'd be mugs. We'd be stupid.

MINNIE: ...the supreme truth...
               ...Of love...

MEN 1:   Give way...
               Minnie deserves love!

MINNIE: ...my brothers...

MEN: We have to.

MEN 1:   Minnie deserves love!

MINNIE: In all the world...

MEN 2:   Minnie deserves love!

MINNIE: ...there's no greater strength...

MEN: Minnie deserves love!

MINNIE: ...than that of love!

ALL: We can't resist. No. No.

The men finally relent and MINNIE *quickly releases* JOHNSON.

SONORA: Your words reminded us what love means.
               Your love is as big as the world!
               In the name of us all – I give him to you.

JOHNSON: Thank you, brothers.

SONORA: Go, Minnie! Get out!

MEN: You'll never return.
               No. Not ever. Not ever.

MINNIE/
JOHNSON: Goodbye, my sweet London.

MEN: No. No more. No. No.
               To return...

MINNIE/
JOHNSON: Goodbye. I'll dream of ya'!

MEN:	Goodbye! Can't bear…to watch.
MINNIE/ JOHNSON:	Goodbye to my sweet London. Goodbye, I'll dream of ya'! To all that I cared for… Forever… Goodbye.
MEN:	You'll never return. No, not ever…
MINNIE/ JOHNSON:	Goodbye my… …dreams of ya'. Goodbye…
MEN:	No, never! Not ever!
MINNIE/ JOHNSON:	*Goodbye! Goodbye!*

MINNIE and JOHNSON continue singing rapturously as they slowly leave the stage.

The men are left alone, in silence.

Blackout.

End of Opera.

WWW.OBERONBOOKS.COM

 Follow us on www.twitter.com/@oberonbooks
& www.facebook.com/oberonbook